# THE EVOLUTION OF ANCIENT HINDUISM

Owing to the antiquity and rarity of this book, certain pages are regrettably absent, and readability is compromised due to the blurring of the original text. If you possess any insights regarding the availability of these missing sections, kindly inform us. Your assistance is crucial in ensuring the completion of this significant work for the benefit of future generations.

# THE EVOLUTION
## OF
# ANCIENT HINDUISM

A. M. FLOYER

GYAN

*Published by*

Gyan Publishing House
5, Ansari Road
Daryaganj, New Delhi-110002
Phone: 011-47034999, 9811692060
E-mail: books@gyanbooks.com

*Distribution Network*
gyanbooks.com
India, USA, Canada, UK, Australia



ISBN: 978-93-6920-004-7 (HB)

First Published, 1888

2nd Impression 2025

*Printed at:* Gyan Press, Delhi.



**THE EVOLUTION OF ANCIENT HINDUISM**
Author: A. M. FLOYER

# THE EVOLUTION

OF

# ANCIENT HINDUISM

# THE EVOLUTION

OF

# ANCIENT HINDUISM

BY

A. M. FLOYER

LONDON: CHAPMAN & HALL

LIMITED

1888

# PART I.—PANTHEISM.

# CHAPTER I.

IT has long been my opinion, that a short history of the evolution of ancient Hinduism, from its primitive form up to its highest development, namely, Buddhism, would prove an interesting study to those who are fond of probing the mysteries and tracing the progress of the human mind. I have therefore taken the labour upon myself, and shall endeavour to point out, as accurately as I can, the main features of this evolutionary process. To attain my object I need not necessarily enter into any details of religious ceremonials, or legends of the gods, because these subjects, however interesting to those who make mythology their special study, are quite subsidiary to the main principles or philosophy of the Hindu religion. It is my intention, therefore, to make use of the researches of others, and merely to glean from them the main facts upon which all scholars are agreed. In dealing with periods of time so long past as 1500 and 2000 years B.C., it is almost unavailing to dispute about the interpretation of any one particular passage or saying; all we can do is to gather the general meaning and tendency of the various traditions, and then piece them together by the aid of common sense and our general knowledge of the characteristics and peculiarities of human nature. I fully admit, therefore, that the theories I am about to offer for consideration are little more than conjectures; but they are, at all events, consistent with facts of which we are certain, and tend to throw some light on a subject which has been frequently and grievously misunderstood.

Before commencing our studies it will be well for us to form a clear notion of the meaning of the word Hinduism. Hinduism is the name of the orthodox religion of the Hindus, an Aryan race which migrated to the banks of the Indus, and gradually spread over that large portion of India now known as Hindustan. It is because Hinduism is the name given to the religion of the Hindu race that I venture, for philosophical purposes, to describe Buddhism as its culmination. Nominally, of course, these two religions are at variance with each other, because Buddha discarded many of the oldest and most cherished of the Hindu traditions; but as Buddha himself and his immediate followers were Hindus by birth, his teaching cannot but be regarded as a phase or development of Hinduism. Besides this, Buddha was the exponent of all that was good in the religion in which he had been educated, rather than a dissentient from it, and as Mr. Rhys Davids says, "Buddhism was the child, the product of Hinduism. Gautama's whole training was Brahmanism; he probably deemed himself to be the most correct exponent of the spirit as distinct from the letter of the ancient faith; and it can only be claimed for him that he was the greatest and wisest and best of the Hindus." It is universally admitted that the first form of Hinduism was a kind of nature-worship, or physiolatry, as it has been termed. That is to say, natural objects, as, for instance, mountains, rivers, and groves, &c., were regarded with superstitious veneration, and worshipped as conscious, almost human deities. Many persons think that, notwithstanding this deification of nature, the Hindus must have brought with them some dim remembrance of pure Monotheism from their home in Central Asia. But if this was so, one cannot help coming to the conclusion, that for a time, at least, all practical belief in a Supreme Being must have died out, otherwise Hinduism could hardly have developed in the manner in which it afterwards did.

That all recognizable belief in God should have been lost is not so extraordinary as it at first sight appears, for when religious teaching was exclusively oral, and the teachers occasionally both credulous and corrupt, we can readily suppose that religion would lose much of its primitive vigour and simplicity, and become insensibly coloured by the prejudices and superstitions of the time. Even in the present day, in spite of our vast literature and the spread of education, how quickly the spirit and essence of truth is obscured, and how much more completely this must have been the case in older times. We see a striking illustration of the manner in which false notions crowd out the fundamental principles upon which they are based in the religious system of the Roman Catholic

Church. In spite of the teaching of the Bible, upon which this faith is founded, the Roman Catholics seem to regard God as an abstract principle, an awful and terrible *Idea* who (or which ?) cannot be approached except through the medium of Jesus Christ; whilst Christ must be approached through the medium of the Virgin Mary or the saints, and in order to secure the patronage of these it is necessary to gain the good offices of the priests. To the masses of the people, therefore, the patron saint seems more real than God or Christ, and the favour of the priest seems the most essential point of all. It is hardly too much to say, perhaps, that had there been no literature and no general education during the past 1800 years, the Roman Catholic religion would have developed into a species of Polytheism before now.

We may therefore very reasonably conclude, that whatever may have been the original belief of the Hindus, it was entirely merged into a system of Polytheism, such as nature-worship at first was. How it came about that the various phenomena of nature should be regarded as divine is a question of much interest, and opinions are greatly divided upon it. Some think that the beauties, the wonders, and the terrors of nature must have made so deep an impression on the minds of the Hindus, that they instinctively wondered and worshipped! It is thought, for instance, that the majestic spectacle of the sun rising morning after morning in the east, and nightly sinking out of sight in the bosom of the west, must have appeared to those ancient people as the stately progressions of a god; whilst the ceaseless flow of the rivers, the mysterious growth of vegetation, and all the strange forms of life with which nature teems, must each and all have claimed the homage of the poetical Hindus. There appear, however, to be many objections to this theory, plausible though it be. In the first place, it is very questionable whether simple, unsophisticated people could have been much impressed by the wonders of nature. All those things to which men are accustomed are accepted as matters of course, besides which, to the ancient Hindus every trivial incident of life was as unaccountable as the grand evolutions of nature. Difficult though it is to realize, it is a fact, that men are apt to be impressed by the various aspects of phenomena in proportion to their knowledge rather than their ignorance. It is a knowledge of the boundless force and the complex systems of nature, rather than the visible results of those forces and laws, which impress us as truly marvellous. Besides which, the more we are able to account for, the more extraordinary does some unaccountable fact become; as, for instance, Darwin would have been much more surprised at the sight of a horned horse than a man totally unacquainted with natural history would be.

I do not think, therefore, that the ancient Hindus could have experienced reverential emotions in their contemplation of nature, any more than an ordinary workman experiences emotional awe as he watches his tobacco kindle, or drops a stone from his hand. Supposing, however, that a few of the intellectual *élite* among the Hindus did observe and marvel at the wonderful objects by which they were surrounded, surely they would have been led to look for the great Maker of all, rather than to deify those objects themselves. Natural phenomena, however magnificent, do not even remotely suggest the possession of mental powers or self-consciousness, and therefore, whatever curiosity the perception of them might awaken, would be most probably directed from themselves to their possible author. It is true that any very unusual occurrence, such as an earthquake, would create a vague feeling of awe and fear, but it is most doubtful whether this fear could in any sense be regarded as a religious emotion. On the whole, the idea that nature-worship was the result of man's instinctive admiration and reverence presents so many difficulties, that I am inclined to think it has no foundation on fact; but if, on the other hand, we accept the less romantic view that nature-worship was at first only a form of ancestor-worship, much that must otherwise remain obscure becomes intelligible. Greatly as we may disagree with some of Mr. Herbert Spencer's conclusions, we may well admit, that in all probability man's first false notions of the supernatural arose from his inability to understand the meaning of death!

The ancients knew that all living creatures are liable to fall into a state of bodily inactivity which we call sleep, and they also knew, from their own personal experiences, that during this state of bodily repose the mind frequently wanders through all kinds of places, and takes part in various scenes and adventures.

The true explanation of dreams not being understood by them, they naturally adopted the supposition that a man has two selves—the self that rests quietly in the hut or tent, and the "other" self that wanders away at will. This was, in fact, the embodiment of the great principle of the existence of spirit as apart from matter, but owing to a natural confusion of ideas the spirit was supposed to be possessed of a second body, just as appears to be the case in dreams. When a man died they believed that his spirit still continued to exist in the second body, under the same conditions as in life; that it might at any time return to reanimate the body which it had deserted, and that in any case he would have the same power to befriend or to injure which he had previously possessed. It was this conviction which gave rise to the notion of ghosts who might be propitiated by offerings and prayers, or offended by neglect. It then followed, as a natural sequence, that if a man was drowned in a stream it was thenceforth believed that

that stream was haunted by his spirit. As time went on, and the individuality of the drowned man was forgotten, his ghost was only remembered as the water-demon, and so on.

By such accidents as these it will easily be understood how, in course of time, the whole of nature might be peopled with ghosts both good and bad—ghosts which were originally thought to be the spirits of the dead, but afterwards only associated with the wood, the river, or the mountain which they were said to haunt.

Mr. Spencer has also pointed out other means by which nature-worship was, or at least may have been, developed. That is, by names given either at birth or in eulogy. For instance, a child born at sunrise was frequently named "Dawn." We can easily suppose that when a person so named came to die, and his ghost propitiated by his descendants for some generations, all knowledge of the individual ancestor or "chief" would gradually be forgotten, and Dawn would be regarded only as the spirit who presided over the sunrise.

Also names given in praise, such as Lionheart, the Serpent, the Bull, and so forth, have been handed down in legends of great men, until at last these descriptive terms have been interpreted literally, and it is believed that men have existed with hoofs like a horse, or horns like a bull. These and many other accidents are sufficient to show how nature-worship may have arisen, and this theory recommends itself to us for many reasons. To begin with, it is an extremely likely and natural explanation of a religion otherwise difficult to account for; but it has greater claims than this to our consideration. To my mind one of the strongest arguments in its support is the belief that these superstitions were founded on the principle of which most people are instinctively convinced, namely, the immortality of the soul. It would seem that every species of religion, no matter how debased and absurd it may have become, has been originally founded upon some truth, and it is this which has kept alive the strangest and most grotesque fancies with which it has been overgrown. It may be compared to a disease which, however corrupt, yet depends for its progress and nourishment upon the life and vitality of the person afflicted by it. That men in old days should have regarded the dead with so much superstition is not at all surprising, when we consider what confusion of thought exists on the subject at the present day. The belief in corporal ghosts, the unreasoning fear of passing through churchyards at night, and so forth, all show us how a belief in the immortality of the soul is mixed and confused with man's inability to comprehend a purely spiritual condition of existence. It is beyond the power of many people to imagine a soul existing without a body, and uninfluenced by mundane conditions ; and if this be so in the nineteenth century, how much more likely the Hindus were to have been misled in the ages of antiquity.

## CHAPTER II.

WHATEVER opinions may be held as to the origin of nature-worship, every one is agreed that this was the earliest form of Hinduism. As (for reasons previously given) I do not think the Hindus had heard of the existence of an Omnipotent Deity, I mark the first step they made towards forming this conception as a transition from physiolatry to the primitive form of Pantheism. At first sight it may appear that Pantheism and physiolatry are synonymous terms, and I shall therefore endeavour to show why a distinction should be made between them. Physiolatry is the adoration of various phases of nature which may have been the mere outgrowth of ancestor-worship, whereas Pantheism is a worship of nature as a whole—the worship of the universe, including the various elements of which it is composed. Physiolatry is essentially polytheistic, whilst Pantheism may be regarded as monotheistic, in tendency at least. If we are curious to know what gave rise to this transition, we must endeavour to picture to ourselves the condition of a people whose mental powers were slowly developing, and then try to imagine how the problems of life would strike them.

We must necessarily suppose that as time went on, and the Hindus became more capable of abstract thought, they would not rest satisfied with a vague belief in a number of gods whom tradition did not represent as being vastly superior to themselves. Moreover, the idea must have occurred to them, that if everything in nature had its double,—if there was a spirit of this and that river and hill, and of the various fruits of the earth,—then surely there must also have existed the spirit or double of the universe itself. This notion was probably not originated by any one man, but was simply the outgrowth of progressive thought. Time begets the power and habit of generalization, and as soon as the Hindus learnt to regard nature as a whole, it seems to me they would be irresistibly drawn to the conclusion that there must be a spirit of the universe, superior to all other spirits, just in proportion as the universe is greater than anything contained within it. It may be that the habit of generalization was developed in the Hindus long before they acquired the power of analogy, but it is pretty certain that the one was the inevitable result of the other, and we can fully understand why some of the oldest Vedic hymns vaguely refer to a prevailing belief in a spirit of the universe. We have now arrived at a period when our studies will be somewhat simplified, because we can go to the Vedas for information ; and it will be well, therefore, at this stage to consider what the Vedas were, and by whom they were taught. The name given by the Hindus to the universal spirit was Brahma, and he was supposed to have entrusted to a few chosen people the Vedas, or unwritten knowledge, directly inspired by himself. These chosen people were called Brahmans, and became at once a select class, or priesthood, whose duty it was to teach the inspired word, and to hand it down orally to their descendants. Thus they acquired a power and position which exists to a great extent even at the present day.

The Brahmans were in fact the intellectual *élite*, the pioneers of thought, who formed themselves into an hereditary priesthood, and naturally acquired habits and modes of thought widely different from the rest of the community. Consequently the terms Brahmanism and Hinduism, although both names of the Hindu religion, became diverse from each other in their practical meaning. The former was a beautiful and subtle philosophy, to which idolatry was but an appendage; Hinduism, on the other hand, being the religion of the masses, was a system of idolatry to which philosophy was but an appendage. In short, we may say that Brahmanism was Pantheism as it presents itself to the minds of the intellectual and refined; whilst Hinduism was Pantheism as it presents itself to the minds of the ignorant, thoughtless, and superstitious.

There is one question which is sure to be asked concerning the Brahmans, namely, how could they suppose that the Vedas which they or their forefathers had composed could possibly be the inspired words of Brahma? It seems to us strange beyond belief that any man, or set of men, could imagine for one moment that their own speculations and convictions were directly inspired. Probably the true answer to this question is, that it was not until long after they were composed, and after they had acquired the venerable dignity of age, that the Vedas were believed to have literally emanated from Brahma. But they might easily be thought to have emanated from him in a metaphorical sense, even by those whose productions they were.

When we remind ourselves how strange and incomprehensible is the origination of a single idea, and that we cannot by any effort of will force a new idea into existence, must we not suppose that in old days they were regarded as heaven-sent? We can therefore believe that men who knew far less than even we do of the phenomena of the human mind, and who were accustomed to attribute every surprising occurrence to some supernatural agency, should have been firmly persuaded, that an idea which flashed upon them was really a revelation, and had been inspired by the essence of all truth and knowledge.

It is probable, therefore, that as a class the Brahmans were honest and intelligent men, who devoted their lives to philosophy and speculation; and when we consider their ignorance of science, together with the many difficulties they had to encounter in the pursuit of knowledge, we cannot but marvel at the vigour of their mental powers, in spite of the discrepancies and superstitions which cling like parasites to their simple and beautiful system.

# CHAPTER III.

In one of the oldest of the Vedic hymns we find an attempt to explain the creation of the universe—

"In the beginning there was neither naught nor aught;
Then was there neither sky nor atmosphere above.
What, then, enshrouded all this teeming universe?
In the receptacle of what was it contained?
Was it enveloped in the gulf profound of water?
Then was there neither death nor immortality;
Only the Existent One breathed calmly, self-contained.
Naught else but He there was—naught else above, beyond.
Then first came darkness hid in darkness, gloom in gloom;
Next all was water, all a chaos indiscreet,
In which the One lay void, shrouded in nothingness.
Then turning inwards, He by self-developed force
Of inner fervour and intense abstraction grew.
First in His mind was formed desire, the primal germ
Productive, which the wise, profoundly searching, say
Is the first subtle bond connecting entity
With nullity."

This dawn of the belief that the universe had been created, is the commencement of what I venture to call the middle form of Pantheism. It shows a far greater tendency towards Monotheism than does the first form of Pantheism, it may be observed, because so much more power and importance is necessarily attached to the Author of all things than to a god who was thought to differ from other gods in degree only and not in kind.

It is not difficult to perceive how it came about that Brahma was believed to be the author of the universe. Nature's wonderful adaptations of means to ends, her sun that rules the day, her stars that steal the gloom from night, her rains that come down to nourish the fruits in her bosom, her ocean tides that ebb and flow obedient to an unknown force, all these marvels, and many more, must ultimately have persuaded the Brahmans (after they had learnt to reflect as well as to observe) that some vast intelligence must have designed and made the whole. This vast intelligence would naturally be ascribed to the chief of their gods, to great nature's double—the self-existent one, Brahma! Brahma, they must have said, has existed before anything that is, was made; nevertheless, he must have contained within himself the essence of all things, because "nothing can be produced out of nothing" (a favourite maxim of the Hindus).

In one sense the verses I have quoted serve as a key to the entire polyglon of Hinduism, for they enable us to understand how it happened that as knowledge grew, and the Hindu religion became more and more complex, the most rationalistic of their thinkers could yet give at least a nominal assent to the most ancient doctrines in the Vedas, because they were so vague that almost any interpretation might be put on them.

Thus, for instance, the lines quoted might be accepted literally, or they might be understood to mean that the essence of what is called the soul, and the essence of what is called the body (or the material) co-existed together through all ages; or it might even be regarded as merely a picturesque description of force acting on matter. We thus see how it was possible for the various schools of Hindu philosophy, widely as they afterwards differed from one another, to be each and all considered orthodox. In this, as in many other instances, we see the tendency of humanity to cling to the letter rather than to the spirit. If a philosopher had declared the Vedas to be a mere collection of verses he would have been considered an infidel, but if he said they must only be taken figuratively, or that they really meant more or less than they appeared to do, he was perfectly welcome to hold his opinions. We, however, cannot doubt but that they who composed the Vedas meant exactly what they said, in the literal sense, and the idea they wished to convey in the verses on the creation must have been somewhat as follows. Brahma is a being from whom emanated the material of which the world is made, and he fashioned it in accordance with his will. He took from himself the essence of the female principle with which he united himself, and from this union proceeded the human race ![1]

Thus was slowly formed the idea of an

[1] This inference is hardly justified by the lines quoted, but the following, taken from the Sama-Veda, shows that this is what is meant—"He caused his own self to fall in twain, and thus became husband and wife. He approached her, and thus were human beings produced."

Omnipotent deity; but, as we shall see, the idea was a very imperfect one. In truth, it is beyond the power of the mightiest intellect to form a clear idea of absolute omnipotence, for however far we may wander in our flights of imagination, we are always bounded by objective experience. We have reason to know that the Hindus regarded the gods, or the doubles of nature, as men like themselves, only more powerful, and having control over physical forces, but by no means independent of physical laws. For instance, they would not suppose that a god could travel at the rate of sixty or seventy miles an hour without wings, but they were quite willing to believe that a god had or might have wings. They would argue, birds have wings, we know not from whence, therefore why should not gods have them? In short, they went by experience. They knew of many wonderful and unaccountable things in nature, and it was not difficult for them to carry the analogy into the spirit world; or, as it would be more correct to term it, the world of fancy. If they saw a caterpillar metamorphosed into a butterfly, it would not seem to them more marvellous that a god should be transformed into an elephant, and we must own that, from their point of view, their reasoning was most plausible. Farther than these analogies led them they did not and could not go; hence we are not surprised to find that their supreme deity, their eternal self-existing one, was a strange medley of power and weakness, of superhuman ability bounded by human frailty—in short, a huge, strong, infinite kind of *man!* Christians may deem it strange that the Hindus should suppose omnipotence limited in power by the laws of nature, but we must remember that Christians base their conceptions of nature on the revelations of God, whereas the ancient Hindus based ther conceptions of God on the revelations of nature. They probably thought that Brahma, being the universal essence, might easily become divested of portions of himself, as a tree may shed its leaves; and having thus permitted matter to emanate from him, besides force, heat, desire, and other motive powers, it would only be another step, implying no supernatural abilities, for the same essence to become the author of the universe, although bound by the nature and sequence of those emanations, just as a man's actions are limited by his inherent, mental, and physical powers.

These theories, however, would hardly account for the existence of mankind. There is something in man, by whatever name it may be called, that makes him differ from the rest of creation, and therefore, they argued, man must have been produced in a different way. To rid themselves of this embarrassing dilemma, the Brahmans were obliged to suppose that Brahma divested himself of the female principle, and thus through marriage with her became the parent of humanity. It may be objected that these conjectural evolutions of thought are too subtle and intricate to bear the stamp of truth upon them; that they represent cunning workmanship rather than the simple results of time and nature. But we must remember that these theories which I have summed up in a few pages are not supposed to be the work of one philosopher, or one generation. On the contrary, we must believe that they were slowly and almost instinctively adopted, because they seemed too obvious to be contradicted. Man has seldom been at a loss to account for beliefs, of the truth of which he is fully persuaded, and the links necessary to connect accepted facts are easily forged out of the imagination.

With regard to the practical philosophy of the ancient Hindus, we find as yet very little to work out, nevertheless a slight change from primitive ideas is noticeable. The first notions of nature-worshippers as to the destiny of man were extremely simple. They believed that the human race, as well as the world itself, was eternal, and that a man's second self, his spirit, must live, whether it deserted the bodily form or not. This spirit, they supposed, would be relatively happy or unhappy according to its conduct on earth, and the degree of favour in which it stood with the gods. It soon became a fixed conviction that the dead went to live in other realms, and thus arose the idea of burning the dead body, so that its double might encompass the spirit in the other world. When, however, the Hindus came to the conclusion that the world was not eternal, but created, and that man was the offspring of Brahma, they were also led to conclude that man must ultimately return to him, and become one with him. This, then, in brief, was the middle form of Pantheism. It was a belief in spirits of nature, and in Brahma as the spirit of the universe, from whom all that is proceeded.

## CHAPTER IV.

We must now turn our attention to what I term the fixed or final form of Pantheism, because, strictly speaking, it is the last evolution of Pantheism which is perceptible in Hinduism, and it is also the crystallized form of the old orthodox Hinduism as distinguishable from the more modern philosophical schools. We have just been studying a monotheistic tendency; we are now about to study a dualistic tendency. We see in the Vedas that the notion of Brahma being the creator of the universe, became merged in the idea that Brahma was himself the universe rather than its author; as if, in fact, the universe were a gigantic organism, of which all the material formed the body and all the spiritual formed the soul. Instead of Brahma having created and fashioned phenomena, it came to be believed that phenomena were a part of himself, existing co-equally with him, as a man's body exists together with his soul. But although every flower of the field was thus thought to be a portion of God, yet it was not supposed to be perfect, or omnipotent, or eternal, any more than the fingers, or the skin, or the hair of a man are identical with him. Man's body is continually growing, changing, and wearing away, every portion of him is in a constant state of renewal, and yet we regard him as the same individual. So of Brahma! The plants, the animals, nay, the world itself is in a continual state of change, growth, maturity, production, and decay, yet the great whole, of which all phenomena are but parts, exists for ever, unchangeable, eternal, so far as man can see. These ideas are beautifully expressed in the following translation from the *Isa Upainshad*—

"Whate'er exists within the universe
Is all to be regarded as enveloped
By the great Lord, as if wrapped in a vesture.
There is one only Being who exists
Unmoved, yet moving swifter than the wind;
Who far outstrips the senses, though as gods
They strive to reach Him; who, Himself at rest,
Transcends the fleetest flight of other beings;
Who like the air supports all vital action.

He moves, yet moves not; He is far, yet near;
He is within the universe."

The same idea is more clearly illustrated in the following lines from the *Bhagavad gitā*—

"I see Thee, mighty Lord of all, revealed
In forms of infinite diversity.
I see Thee, like a mass of purest light,
Flashing Thy lustre everywhere around.
I see Thee crowned with splendour like the sun,
Pervading earth and sky immeasurable;
Boundless, without beginning, middle, end;
Preserver of imperishable law,
The everlasting Man!"

We may well ask ourselves how those who could compose anything so beautiful as the above poetry, and whose notions of God were at least refined and elevated, could yet have sanctioned, still less believed, in the inferior and gross gods of Hindu mythology. The reason is in all probability not far to seek. We know from our own experience how difficult it is to free ourselves from old habits of thought; and the traditions of our childhood are not easily displaced. Sentiment lingers around customs and actions which reason has long ago condemned, and the curfew bell still rings in our ears with a warning sound, although the law with which it is associated has long since passed away. It is comparatively easy to progress in philosophy provided that the new can be grafted on the old, but it is almost impossible to abolish the old at the introduction of the new.

These considerations, united with others of a more selfish or prudential kind, would render it very hard even for the most advanced philosopher to cast away his gods. How much more so then would it be for the common people? Those uneducated masses who could not help degrading a religion to their own level,—men who could only understand and care for a system of rewards and punishments, and of securing the best terms for themselves that they conveniently could,—these would naturally cling to superstition with all the stubborn tenacity of ignorance. So long, therefore, as the gods satisfied the religious demands of the people, the people would uphold them, and bitterly denounce those who hinted that they were myths. Thus upon this question sentiment, expediency, and bigotry would join hands together for the purpose of upholding the old *régime;* whilst

D

reason, ever ready to become a partisan, would soon suggest some new method of reconciling philosophy with superstition.

The dualistic theories with regard to Brahma caused a slight but inevitable change of opinion concerning the origin and destiny of man. The notion that the human race was the offspring of Brahma came to be believed metaphorically only, and simply meant that the union of the spiritual and material produced mankind. Man was therefore thought to be derived from, but not born of, Brahma, his body being a portion of eternal matter, and his soul a portion of the soul of the universe. One great distinction, however, seems to have been made between the condition of God and man. Brahma was completely dual, spirit and body existing together, united indeed, but not fused into one; whilst man was regarded as a mixture of spiritual and material, or animal qualities. Brahma's existence, according to these views, might be illustrated by two distinct circles which just touched each other, whereas man might be compared to two circles, one encompassed by the other; and it was this environment of spirit in matter which (in the opinion of the Hindus) was the origin of evil. Man's soul, once pure and godlike, became obscured, it was thought, by its imprisonment in the flesh, because mere matter is ignorant and gross. To separate himself as much as possible from all material pleasures and interests was therefore considered the proper object of a man's life. This idea gave rise to the most exaggerated notions about the necessity of self-torture, and the efficacy of bodily suffering. It was believed that the body, together with the physical desires attributed to it, was necessarily opposed to the soul which dwelt within it, and that an unceasing warfare between the two was unavoidable. In old days, as at the present time, it was very difficult not to believe that distinctions made for practical use are not arbitrary and final. We all know that there is a difference between body and spirit; but if we forget their inter-dependence on each other, we commit a blunder which may cause much unhappiness in life. This blunder the Hindus unconsciously made! They taught that the spiritual could be cultivated by the suppression of the physical, never recognizing that the one has its roots in the other.

About 500 years B.C., or rather before, the doctrine of the transmigration of souls was taught. It found favour, no doubt, on account of its explanation of the inequalities of life. If a man was born blind as a punishment for sins committed in a previous life, the apparent injustice of nature was explained away.

A few words must be added here on the subject of those horrible sacrificial rites which have been extensively practised by the Hindus. We have reason to believe that the Brahmans were averse to these sacrifices, partly on humanitarian grounds, and partly because of the inconsistency of offering to the gods portions of Brahma. But sacrificial rites were congenial to the people, and chiefly on this account they were maintained. Why the people should be so fond of offering sacrifices seems strange, but we must remember that they had always been used to them. In the days of ancestor-worship, food was offered to the spirits of the dead, because it was supposed that they required food as much as did the living men. These offerings were, of course, acts of propitiation, and the idea took such deep root in the minds of the uneducated, that persuasion and philosophy were alike unable to overcome it.

We have now obtained a bird's-eye view of Hindu Pantheism in its final condition, before it became merged into different philosophical schools.

Shortly before the advent of Buddha there was a period of great intellectual activity among the Brahmans, and they were anxious to form clearer and more scientific views of religion and ethics. This spirit of inquiry resulted in the formation of six orthodox schools of philosophy. It is not known whether these schools were actually established before Buddha began to teach, but it is highly probable that they were. In any case, however, the different opinions were known and discussed in his time, and many of them were incorporated into his own philosophy.

From an evolutionary point of view, the only school of importance is the Vedanta, because it is the one connecting link between the old pantheistic Hinduism and Buddhism. To speak scientifically, Vedantism was a new species, whilst the other schools were but varieties, of the old Hinduism.

It is to the study of this school, therefore, that I propose to devote the whole of the next part.

# PART II.—VEDANTISM.

## CHAPTER V.

THE Vedantist school of thought was founded some five or six centuries B.C., and owed its origin to a philosopher named Bādarāyana. The precise date when this school was formed is, as I have said, a matter of uncertainty, but the question is not one of much importance to us. The ideas of which it was the embodiment are shadowed forth in the Upanishads, and must therefore have existed for some time before Bādarāyana put them into definite shape.

Our knowledge of the growth and development of the Vedanta is so scanty, that we shall frequently be obliged to supplement our information by drawing upon our common sense. We know that the Brahmans attained great wisdom and the power of abstract thought, hence when we come to consider theories of theirs, which appear to be full of contradictions and absurdities, we must not rest satisfied, as some are content to do, and say, "What follies these ancient philosophers were capable of." We must feel assured that however mistaken the Brahmans were, at all events they could not have been the dupes of vulgar and transparent errors. There must then be something more plausible in these apparently conflicting doctrines than we are at first sight able to perceive, and we may well ask ourselves what is the explanation of them?

This great question I have endeavoured to solve, but I am conscious of having done so very imperfectly, and much yet remains to be done.

Our first consideration must of course be the nature and attributes of Brahma according to the Vedanta; everything hinges upon this! In the Vedanta Brahma is defined as "that from which the production of this universe results." This does not appear to differ from the original theory (explained in Part I.) of the ancient Hindus, who described Brahma as the universal essence from whom all things originally emanated. Other portions of the Vedanta show us, however, that something more than this was intended, because we are told that the eternal *soul* of the Universe exists only, and that all else, including the material world, is illusion. The Pantheistic school regarded matter, force, &c., &c., as things, and they appear first to have considered Brahma's creation of the world as simply a piece of magnificent manipulation, and afterwards that it was the corporeal part of him.

We gather that the Vedanta went much further than this; that it was, in fact, the precursor of the comparatively modern notion that everything material is only phenomena, and that we know nothing of the "thing in itself," as Kant has termed it, which lies behind phenomena.

So far as I can understand it, the Vedanta teaches that Brahma was neither a manipulator, nor a type of man whose body and soul constituted a dual existence, but that he was merely the embodiment of ideas. By this I mean, that they believed the world to be composed of matter, and matter when analyzed is theoretically "a fortuitous concourse of atoms," and atoms being absolutely indivisible are simple ideas. It was matter as an idea, therefore, that was a part of the essence of Brahma. Again, heat is only an idea in one sense. Latent heat exists in every stick that straws the ground, but it only becomes phenomenal under certain favourable circumstances. Weight is another phenomenon which owes its existence to an ideal power, the attraction of gravitation. Of course it will be said at once that the knowledge we have of the attraction of gravitation, latent heat, &c., &c., was not possessed by the Hindus at the time of which I am writing, and therefore the Vedanta could not be supposed to allude to them. But I think systems may be shadowed forth ages before man has been able to find any scientific ground for them. For instance, we can imagine that an ancient philosopher might have defined weight as the power of appearing heavy, and this power would certainly have ranked as an idea. Again, if we argue from nature, we see that under certain conditions an acorn will become an oak, but a pebble under the same condition will never become one. We see also that warmth and moisture produce widely different results when applied to different specimens of animal and vegetable life.

Maize does not blossom into roses, grasses do not become vines, palms do not produce dates, and so on. Thus the existence and development of all things are dependent upon some quality or potentiality inherent in each, and these qualities are ideas, or, as the Vedantists would say, they are God! He was "what gold is to a bracelet," "what curds are to whey," and we may add, what vitality is to organic life.

Again, we see reflected on the surface of a lake the trees that line its banks, and the sky above,—we see, in fact, a representation of natural scenery, but we know that it is a representation only; metaphorically speaking, this was the Vedantist's notion of the material world! Neither the world nor the reflections cast on a lake are absolutely illusion, for they both actually exist, but inasmuch as they are not "things in themselves," only things as they appear to us, they are illusive. Visible nature, therefore, was not Brahma according to the Vedantists, but he was the reality which lay behind it, the motive power which permitted and regulated its being. Once more, the Brahmans saw as we see the change from life to death. A living organism, be it man, or beast, or tree, is full of marvellous capacities for movement, growth, and development; but there comes a time when all these cease to be, when the most active, intelligent of organisms becomes senseless, motionless, dead! What has brought about this strange transition? What is that which has been lost?

Nothing visible, nothing tangible, nothing that can be replaced. It is not the blood of the animal or the sap of the tree that has been lost, but the power to circulate it, and give it warmth and vitality,—this is what is wanting. Thus in a philosophic sense life, the most real and forcible phenomena that we know, owes its existence to an ideal power.

Such reflections as these might easily have been made, as we have seen, after simple observations of nature, without any aid from natural science, or the wisdom of the nineteenth century.

## CHAPTER VI.

WE have now to consider the theories of the Vedanta concerning the strictly spiritual aspect of Brahma—a question full of difficulties, and one which we cannot pretend to understand except in a very incomplete manner.

It is, however, *the* question of all others in Vedantism, the most worthy of study, as it embodies the highest and boldest flights of the human imagination.

The creed of the Vedantist briefly stated was as follows. The subjective or spiritual side of Brahma was to man what matter is to the Universe, what force and vitality are in relation to their manifestations in nature. The old school of Hindus believed, as we have seen, that man was a type of God,—that the one was simply a magnified edition of the other. The Vedantists regarded God as a pure idea, a vast potentiality.

He was pure intelligence without reason, pure knowledge without thought, pure consciousness without individuality, pure joy without desire, perfect happiness without attainment or object, perfect love without anything to love, and Omnipotence without volition.

These definitions certainly read like a string of contradictions, a mass of utter absurdity, and as such they are apt to be regarded by modern scholars. But the extremely patent absurdity of these ideas should teach us that we must look below the surface to see if some hidden meaning has not been attached to them. Let it be our task to discover what that meaning was, or at least what it may have been. To begin with, let us ask ourselves how it is conceivable that intelligence could exist without reason, or knowledge without thought? We must first call to mind the different conditions which might presumably exist between Brahma and man. Man comes into the world ignorant of all things, but with the aid of purely physical qualities, that is, with the aid of nerves, brain, senses, &c., he is enabled to learn bit by bit, and then by reasoning upon this knowledge gained, he attains more. Thus to man reason and thought are the necessary accompaniments of intelligence and knowledge, and therefore man jumps to the conclusion that these accompaniments would always be necessary under all circumstances. Reason, however, is to the intelligence what spectacles are to the near-sighted, that is to say, it helps man to atone for a natural defect, it gives him in an indirect manner the knowledge which an unobscured and perfect intelligence would perceive directly without extraneous aid. Here was the great difference which the Vedantists saw between Brahma and man. If Brahma was himself the essence of all knowledge, he could not require those methods of acquiring it which are necessary to man. Our own experience teaches us that we have no need to reason about a thing that we know—as, for instance, we all know that we perceive without any aid from reason; on the contrary, this is the one great incontrovertible fact upon which reason takes her stand. This being the case, the Vedantists were not illogical in supposing that Brahma must be independent of the human aids of thought and reason.

A more difficult problem to solve is, how they could suppose Brahma to be pure consciousness without the consciousness of "I and thou!" Here again we must remind ourselves of the natural environment by which we are limited, if we would understand what consciousness might be, unconnected with a human organization. To be conscious of "I and thou" is the first proof of any consciousness at all in creatures who possess separate individuality; but for Brahma, who was believed to be the only real entity, there could be no sense of more than "I," because for him no "thou" existed.

We must remember also, that in the opinion of the Vedantists Brahma was wholly subjective, a state unattainable to man. The highest idealism, the most unreal dreamland, the wildest flights of imagination, all rest on man's objective experiences, because no ideas can be recognized by him until made manifest through the medium of phenomena. Beauty has no meaning for us unless made visible to us, and even our preferences for certain colours and forms are dependent upon our nerves, and physical organization generally. To us, therefore, a purely subjective existence is one which we can hardly even imagine. Brahma, however, was supposed to possess feeling without the necessity of any object to occasion it; he was conscious of things in themselves, without the aid of phenomena. To such a being (if he existed) consciousness would simply be an intense realization of himself and his own attributes. Such a state can be pictured by us in a feeble degree, if we recall the sensations we have occasionally experienced when under the spell of some great mental enjoyment. Those, for instance, who appreciate music, know that there are moments when all consciousness of I and thou disappears, when objective individuality is forgotten, and when time, place, and circumstance seem to vanish like a dream, having only the supreme consciousness of infinite enjoyment. Yet this is no state of hazy dreamland, of mental repose; on the contrary, never does consciousness seem more vivid, never does the mind seem more vigorous, than when for a time the shackles that bind us to material life are shaken off, and we are free.

Those who have at any time experienced the feelings to which I have alluded, can imagine vaguely what might be the realization of consciousness attributed to Brahma; for if we know the buoyancy of air, we can understand how keenly enjoyable a purer medium might be.

The next question is, how can pure joy be possible without desire, or happiness without change, progression, or attainment?

This of course seems to us a contradiction in terms, because to us the goal of joy and happiness, though always striven for, is never attainable.

> "Earth will never meet the heaven,
> Never can the There be Here!"

Progression is the only criterion of our success, therefore, and becomes the essential element of our happiness. But if we ask ourselves for what we are striving—what is that dim and distant goal which is almost hidden from us even in our dreams?—we cannot fail to see that desire and progress have there no place. So far as we *can* perceive it, the goal of happiness is simply the feeling of intense joy, quite apart from the things that produce that feeling. Nothing in this world is actually pleasure or happiness, but only the means to gain these ends, whilst ideal delight is one long realization of happiness which needs no medium to procure it. We have all of us experienced the fact that a pleasurable occupation sometimes gives us no gratification, whilst, on the other hand, there are times when we have a keen sense of enjoyment for which we find it difficult to account. Of course we are aware that this uncertainty of response to stimulus, as we may call it, is dependent upon our physical health and mental serenity; but the fact should teach us that no form of pleasure is a pleasure in itself. Music, poetry, painting, and other things are precious to us, because it is only through them that we are able to perceive the ideas which they embody.

If we are able to realize what I have been stating, we must see that we need go only one step further to understand how it might be supposed that Brahma might be the essence of love without having an object of affection.

Love is in the purest sense an intense delight in union, a desire to join, through sympathy, the individual feelings. To be "at one" with a person is an expression often used to signify that blending together, or unity, of which people of high organization are capable.

Brahma was therefore the very type of love. To be the harmonious essence of all things and to feel all things was to be of necessity the fountain of love, or, to speak more correctly, he was of all love the pure idea which required no object to make it manifest.

Two more considerations yet remain before us. The first is, how could Brahma be Omnipotence without volition? Of all questions, perhaps, that of the freedom of the will, together with the many side issues involved in it, is one upon which it is the most difficult for people to agree. If there is one thing more distinctly impressed upon our consciousness than another, it is the belief that our wills are free, and thus we find it almost impossible to imagine Omnipotence without volition. There are many people, however, who hold that no man's will is really free, but that he is bound to obey his strongest motive, whatsoever it may be. Volition, they say, is but the name for the preponderant motive which decides his actions, and all he can boast of possessing, more than "the vexed straw on the wind," is, that his stimulus to movement proceeds from a mental and not a physical compulsion.

Such theories as these must have been in the minds of the Vedantists when they ascribed Omnipotence to Brahma without volition. They must have meant that everything which existed, even in this illusive world, was in accordance with the nature of Brahma; but as he neither reasoned, nor was even aware of the existence of phenomena, he was conscious of no wish or will concerning it. To put the same idea into other words, it might be said, that things occur and exist in accordance with the nature and potentiality of the ideas which lie behind them, without being consciously and arbitrarily decreed. Brahma, as the personification of pure ideas, was supposed to influence the universe, just as the nerves or lungs of a man influence his being, namely, in strict conformity with his physique, but without requiring his concurrence, and quite independent of his volition. Such at least we must suppose to have been the opinions of the Vedantists.

## CHAPTER VII.

I SUSPECT that no one can have read the preceding chapter without feeling that, explain as we may, the Brahma of the Vedanta is not only a vague, but an unsatisfactory creation of the imagination, and that his attributed qualities do not tally with the character accorded to him.

It will be asked, perhaps, how could Brahma be perfect knowledge, and yet absolutely unaware of the existence of phenomena? How are we to account for the origin of evil and pain, if everything that is, is of Brahma? How are we to imagine that the source of all consciousness could be unconscious of ourselves?

To these questions I cannot undertake to give the correct answers, but I can at all events offer a few suggestions. With regard to the limits of pure knowledge, we must remind ourselves that if Brahma was purely subjective, his attributes would also be subjective. Absolute knowledge of what lies behind phenomena, of the eternal ideas which control the world, was believed to be his, but he had no cognizance of illusory appearances. To see things as man sees them, to be aware of such facts as individuality and thought, it would be necessary, they would suppose, to become as man, that is, to see with human eyes, and to feel with individualized self-consciousness, to be bound up, in fact, in objective appearances. To a nature such as the Vedantists imputed to Brahma this was an impossibility, because it implies contradiction. For a harmonious whole to be at the same time an isolated part, for pure knowledge to mistake illusions for realities, is entirely unthinkable, from a Hindu point of view, at all events.

In short, according to the Vedanta, Brahma was not a god at all, either personal or impersonal, but was in truth *an ideal state of being!* Brahma was the Paradise that lay the other side the great river, and perfect though that land might be, it yet gave no aid to those who desired to reach it. No generous branches stretched across the stream for man to grasp, no shadowy skiff haunted the banks to carry weary souls safe to the haven of rest. Absolutely perfect, absolutely impassive, the Vedantist's paradise could only be gained by man's endeavour, and his salvation depended on his love for God (which means his desire for eternal happiness), and not, as Christianity teaches, on God's love for man.

But although Brahma was only another name for heaven, the Hindu was not content with the hope of entering it, he desired himself to become it,—he desired not only to live with Brahma, but to be him. Thus to lose all individuality, and be merged in pure ideas, oblivious of all human ties, does not appear to us a very attractive goal; and greatly as the Hindus might revere Brahma as the essence of all that is grand and good, we cannot think that to become one with him would be particularly desirable. There seems to be nothing in this cold, solitary, impassive existence to make any one long to share it. Yet we know that this desire has been so strongly felt, that many have suffered tortures for it, and given up life gladly as a worthless thing compared to it.

## CHAPTER VIII.

WE must now fix our attention upon what the Vedanta taught concerning man, his relationship to Brahma, and his code of ethics. Man, the Vedantists considered, was a dual creature, being on the one hand tangible, changeable, and objective, and on the other hand, being an emanation from Brahma, he was immutable, pure, and perfect. Body and soul were two distinct things which were united together, or rather the one was shrouded in the other. In the more ancient forms of Hinduism we have seen that the soul was supposed to mean the entire mental nature, all that is not represented by the corporeal existence. The Vedantists went farther than this. They held that even the mental faculties and individual character were a part of physical life, and perished with the body. All that a man is, or thinks he is, was considered to be mere illusion, like all other phenomena, the only external portion of the man being his potentiality and consciousness. To quote a well-known writer, "the living soul of individuals, when separated off from the supreme soul, is regarded as enclosed in a succession of cases which envelop it, and, as it were, fold over the other like the coats of an onion."

The whole question of identity is indeed one so difficult to understand, that it is no wonder the Vedanta offers little more than vague terms, and identity without memory, consciousness without self-consciousness, the soul without intellectual faculties, present problems which are entangled in a thick network of possibilities which it would be vain to enter upon here. We are bound to conclude that self-consciousness was not believed to be the same thing as a sense of identity, but simply as the accidental result of individual life, a sense of isolation, caused by material environment, in place of ideal unity. It may be objected that a true sense of existence, *i. e.* absolute consciousness, implies memory, and that even if the soul "hath elsewhere its setting," the "birth" and the "forgetting" have practically broken the cord of connection. But the Vedantists did not seem to consider the loss of memory as any obstacle to their conscious enjoyment. Indeed, to them memory was a fetter which bound them to their isolated life in the prison house of the flesh, and they eagerly looked forward to the time when they should fling it off for ever, and enter the region of pure idea.

The ethics of the Vedanta were singularly simple, as we shall see.

Since the object of life was to fit man for absorption into Brahma, all efforts were to be directed towards that end. The idea that any good might be obtained by a wise and moderate enjoyment of life's pleasures did not enter into this scheme. Earthly life was considered a delusion and a misery, worth absolutely nothing except as a means of obtaining happiness hereafter. Thus, strangely enough, the adoration of nature led the Hindus at last to despise nature, and a belief in the beauty and perfection of her laws consisted contemporaneously with an indifference to the results of those laws. They looked from nature to God, and then treated with contempt the basis upon which their theology was built. To become fit for absorption these philosophers taught that man must rid himself of all those things which had rendered possible his separation from Brahma. Entrance upon human existence was considered the cause of the abstraction of the soul from him, and the cause of all pain and ignorance, but at the same time, it was only through living an earthly life in a holy state that the soul could be purified sufficiently to admit of its ultimate reunion. Suicide, therefore, was out of the question, because the soul would be left in the same impure and clogged condition after death as before, and have still to work out its redemption in some other individual existence. A living death, however, was not considered equally fruitless. On the contrary, the mortification of the body, and the denial of those mental and physical desires which are bound up with it, was thought to be meretorious and proper. In fact, the physical nature was treated like a poor despicable jade who has work to perform, but who receives no honour or commendation for its performance. Some of the people, reputed holiest, lived sad, solitary lives, and tortured themselves in various ways, whilst all believed in the theory of entire self-sacrifice, whether they practised it or not.

Mistaken though these ideas are, and wholly repugnant to our feelings, they are not without a more pleasing side. The belief in the efficacy of self-torture is at least preferable to a belief in the efficacy of torturing others, and a Hindu devotee is a more edifying spectacle than the flames of the Inquisition, for instance. Another fact is well worthy of remark, namely, the tolerance of the Hindu spirit. They recognized the fact that men are not all born equal, either in position or disposition, and therefore that the same results could not be expected from all. The philosophical Brahman who eschewed the world, and who was able to soar upwards towards Brahma in his dreams and aspirations, was of course considered specially holy; but the practical, uneducated tiller of the soil, or drawer of water, whose imaginative mind could rise no higher than the worship of the gods, and who built his hopes upon good works, that is, upon fair dealing and almsgiving, &c., &c., was still encouraged to persevere. For him the way to God was a long one, but still he could look forward to reaching eventually the desired goal. Even the outcasts and sinners were believed to be following, although afar off, for sin was thought to be the spawn of ignorance and delusion, rather than the deliberate choice of evil made by an innately vicious heart.

In taking leave of Vedantism, it will surely be well for us to extend to the ancient Hindus the same tolerance of spirit which they extended to others. We know that there was much in the vulgar form of their religion which was absurd and even brutal, but behind the common form lay deep and beautiful ideas which we cannot but admire. More than all, we know that there were many men among them who searched after truth with a devotion and singleness of purpose which may well serve as a beacon light to us all.

# PART III.—BUDDHISM.

# CHAPTER IX.

IT would be almost impossible to form any clear idea of Buddhism without some slight knowledge of the life and history of Buddha. I shall, however, content myself with quoting the main facts only concerning him, not only because many people are already familiar with the story of his life, but also because much that is interesting from a biographical point of view would be quite superfluous for those who wish simply to gain an insight into his philosophy.

Buddha was born about six hundred years B.C., and was the son of Suddhodana, the raja of the Sākyas. With the legends which surround his birth and early life we need not deal, for we know very few reliable facts about him until he reached his twenty-ninth year, when he made up his mind to leave his dearly-loved young wife and child, in

F 2

order to devote himself to religion, or rather philosophy. Buddha was undoubtedly one of those men who are born far in advance of their time—one of those great spirits who, in spite of personal and domestic happiness, are yet tormented by the knowledge of the sufferings of others; a man to whom the problems of life, pain, and death assume an importance of the highest magnitude, his own individual prosperity and pleasure counting as nothing. We can easily understand also that popular Hinduism, as distinguished from Brahmanism, was a source of dissatisfaction to him. The worship and sacrifices offered to vulgar and insatiable gods were revolting, and he naturally craved for some higher knowledge and nobler belief.

At the age of twenty-eight years he therefore made up his mind to forsake his home, and withdraw into the jungle. He there remained for six years, in the company of five disciples, with whom he fasted and did penance, according to the Hindu doctrines, which taught the efficacy of suffering in freeing the soul from the vile fetters of the body. During those six years Buddha no doubt studied the philosophy of Vedantism, as well as the other schools of orthodox Hinduism, and from those studies he gathered the fundamental principles of the new religion which he afterwards taught. At the end of his sixth year of penance Buddha found that although he had fasted, and mortified himself in order to be more fit for unity with God, yet he was in no way the better for it. His body was not subdued, his soul not elevated—all had been in vain.

He then despaired of deriving any benefit from a continuance of the same course of life, and began to take sufficient food, giving up at the same time all forms of penance. Whilst thus emaciated, weary, weak, and disappointed, his disciples deserted him, for in their opinion he had succumbed to temptation, and was no longer worthy to be their leader.

Being thus abandoned by his companions, overwhelmed with a sense of failure, not knowing what his next step should be, and entirely without that sense of peace and beatitude which penance was believed to produce, he became grievously afflicted with sorrow. The story of his assailment, his conflict, and final victory is poetically regarded by his devoted followers of after days as a material one, a battle of thews and sinews, but in reality it was of course a mental conflict. He was not only distracted by doubts and difficulties, but apparently there came upon him one of those violent upheavals of the inner nature which I can only describe as a nerve-storm. It was a kind of passionate ebullition, a whirlwind of feeling, which for the time being wrenches a man adrift from his moral anchors and flings him about in mad gyrations, until at last the storm seems spent through its own vehemence.

It is one thing to fail to achieve through frailty of purpose, or to lose sight of our end through our own negligence, but it is widely different, and far more painful, to find that, in spite of unwearying devotion, toil, and watchfulness, the end is no nearer, the goal no more sure. This was Buddha's condition when this terrible nerve-storm overtook him. But after the storm came the calm, and whilst sitting under the Bo tree, he saw his way towards formulating a new philosophy, a philosophy which has been briefly summed up as "the power over the human heart of inward culture, and of love to others." People often regard Buddha as the author of a wholly new religion, but this was not the case, and if we try to study it as such, we find it exceedingly difficult, if not impossible, to understand. But if, on the other hand, we are convinced that Buddha was an orthodox Hindu of the Vedantist school of thought on every subject upon which he does not express a difference of opinion, all that is perplexing and contradictory can be explained away.

I do not think that Buddha ever questioned the abstract truths of Brahmanism ; his attention was directed entirely to moral philosophy, and to the purification of his religion from the corruptions which the vulgar and superstitious had nourished within it.

During that time of calm reflection under the Bo tree, Buddha must have thought out almost the whole of his philosophy, because from that time forward he devoted himself entirely to its promulgation as a man only could who had no doubts left concerning its truth and importance.

## CHAPTER X.

Now that we are about to take into consideration the main principles of Buddha's philosophy, we instinctively turn our attention first towards his theories concerning the Supreme Deity, and we learn with surprise, that no omniscient God has *any* place in his religious system. This fact will cease to surprise us, however, if we take it for granted that Buddha was strongly imbued with the spirit of Vedantism, for, as we have seen, the Vedantists denied that Brahma was a personal deity, or had any cognizance of human life. Presumably Buddha acquiesced in the statement that such a being existed, but declined to give to him (or it?) the name of God. He probably recognized the fact, that the physical attributes of Brahma were simply laws of nature of which we know nothing, save when manifested through the medium of phenomena, and which are therefore of no interest to us except when thus manifested.

With regard to the spiritual side of Brahma, he must have seen, as we see, that pure love, consciousness, joy, and so forth are but conditions of existence, and in no sense do they embody the essentials of a deity. He seems to have taken the same view as a more modern philosopher who says, that if a god is to be of any interest to us, he must be a personal one. I shall presently hope to show that Buddha did not disbelieve in the existence of ideal happiness, but for the moment it is only necessary to point out that this ideal was not regarded by him as a god. With reference to the gods in general, he admitted their reality; for he believed that other worlds—places both of enjoyment and torment—had been evolved in the same manner as this world, and that they were inhabited by creatures of the same genus as man, but perhaps superior, who went by the name of gods, but he did not believe that they had any power over the destinies of men. Man was alone responsible for himself to himself; no good angel could raise him, neither could any evil fiend drag him downward. Hence all prayers and sacrifices were abolished by true Buddhists, as being not only superfluous, but revolting to the true dignity of mankind.

This theory of course must have had great charms for the Hindus. So many must have been led to fancy that it was of no use to try to combat fortune if the gods appeared to be against them, and thus by this very hopelessness rendering themselves doubly unfortunate. But when they were taught to rely on themselves, and to defy the fates, who were powerless to harm them, a feeling of renewed life and energy must have animated them.

We are now on the threshold of perhaps the most puzzling of Buddhist doctrines, namely, the origin of man, his nature, and his future. I use the word puzzling, because we find some of Buddha's clearest and most emphatic statements seem to be in direct contradiction to the main principles of his teaching. This being the case, we must endeavour to read between the lines, and thus reconcile if we can the conflicting evidence. To begin with, I believe it is an indisputable fact, that Buddha denied the immortality of the soul. He taught in plain language that man is but a synthesis of certain objects and forces, as a chariot is but the combination of certain other objects and forces, and that when these materials are disunited, the chariot, as such, is destroyed, the man, as such, is annihilated. No materialist could preach the destructibility of all individual things or creatures more emphatically than did Buddha. As to the soul, he asserted positively, that there was no such thing at all, even during a man's life, still less after his death. On the other hand, however, if he really meant what his words imply, his moral precepts, his theories concerning transmigration, and of Nirvāna, appear to be wholly inconsistent with his convictions.

The time has not yet come for us to consider what his moral philosophy was, but we shall presently see that his teaching everywhere implied that this life is but a preparation, and not a consummation. Those who believe that Buddha was nothing more or less than a materialist, find no stumbling-block to their theory in his ethics, because they say any infidel may have good principles and moral qualities. This is of course perfectly true. An atheist or materialist may preach the doctrine of kindness, justice, and rectitude, but his reasons for advocating these are and must be based on the conviction, that the exercise of such qualities would augment the sum of man's happiness in this world. Buddha, on the contrary, called upon men to renounce many enjoyments which were so innocent in themselves, as in no way to detract from the sum of human happiness. If all life ends for the individual when the heart ceases to beat, then surely there could be no harm in a man's enjoying pleasures which could not bring retribution on himself or others. But Buddha despised many innocent pleasures, solely on the ground that they tended to make human life too agreeable, a most unreasonable doctrine, merely from a materialist's point of view. If, however, he believed that a love of individual life here prevented a man's attaining far more complete happiness in the future, he was perfectly logical. Some people think he considered it unadvisable to enjoy the pleasures of life because there is always a possibility of being deprived of them. This appears to be a somewhat far-fetched notion ; and if Buddha had been led to hold such an opinion, how can we account for the fact that he encouraged the growth of all loving and kindly feelings? If the object of life is to avoid pain, then we ought to stifle all feelings of a warmer nature than mere good-natured tolerance; knowing how much we can be made to suffer through loving others.

Apart from this, how could a pure materialist believe in the transmigration of souls? Undoubtedly Buddha did not believe that a man (*i. e.* all those qualities and characteristics which together make up the individual) could leave his body at death and enter another body; but he must have believed that the result of a man's life would continue after his death, and that this result called Karma would influence a new birth. Karma was, in fact, a heritage.

But this was not all. Buddha believed that the transmigration of souls was a system of justice, an exemplification of the truth, that a man must reap what he has sown. Now surely if there was nothing of the original man except the harvest of his actions transmitted to the newly-born inheritor of them, where is the justice? Why should an innocent child be branded with a disease which was the fruit of evil wrought by a totally different person? Or why should a man lead an exemplary life for the sake of benefiting some alien creature to be born after him? Of course, from a perfectly unselfish point of view, a man might be willing to lead a life of self-denial in order to transmit a good Karma to some one else; but Buddha does not seem to have founded his religion on any principle of absolute unselfishness. On the contrary, he was continually impressing upon his hearers that the object of life was to secure ultimate happiness, and get rid of all pain. What, then, was the eternal thread which he must have believed to exist through all forms of life, and which might eventually arrive at the perfection of bliss, Nirvāna? We should of course answer, the soul, if he had not declared that all belief in a soul was heresy. What, then, could it be? The only way of escaping this difficulty is by remembering the class of people whom he was addressing, and the nature of the religion he was attempting to reform. He was teaching the Hindus who held by the old pantheistic doctrines, and not the Vedantist school, which came into existence but a short time previous to himself. Now we have seen that the old school probably believed the soul to be an indestructible individuality, therefore I think that when Buddha said there was no such thing as a soul, he used the word in the old-fashioned sense, meaning to say, that as a man's individuality is dependent on circumstances, it could not be immortal or indivisible. Nevertheless, there is strong reason for the presumption that he accepted fully the Vedantist belief in the immortality of the consciousness. He believed, no doubt, that an undying spark of godlike consciousness kindled the flame to which life has been compared, and that when death overtakes the individual, this same spark, still encumbered with the Karma of the departed being, is forced again and again to enter upon individual life, until, by the aid of mortal endeavour, the immortal shall at last regain its freedom, and exist for ever in bliss.

## CHAPTER XI.

Supposing that the conclusions arrived at in the preceding chapter are correct, we may sum up the philosophy of Buddha in a few words.

He believed with the Vedantists in the real existence of pure love, joy, and consciousness, and he believed that from this ideal existence emanated the conscious vitality which animates the living creature, and that its imprisonment in mutable life was the source of all sufferings; therefore the more a man could wean himself from a love of physical life, the sooner would the vital spark regain its original condition of ideal happiness.

If it be taken for granted that this is the outline of Buddha's creed, we shall see how admirably his ethical teaching was adapted to the object which he had in view. It will be remembered that Hindu orthodoxy divided

the people into two classes, the Brahmans and non-Brahmans. To the former belonged philosophy, leisure, and many privileges, whilst the vocation of the latter class was that of the uneducated soldier or citizen. Buddha made the same broad distinction, but on an altered basis. The orthodox Brahmans were a hereditary priesthood, or aristocracy, and the gulf that separated them from the common people was impassable. Buddha, on the contrary, believed in natural selection, and thought little of the accidents of birth. The following verses from the Buddhist scriptures prove this unmistakably—

> "Not by birth does one become low caste,
> Not by birth does one become a Brahman;
> By his actions alone one becomes low caste,
> By his actions alone one becomes a Brahman."

In short, Buddha recognized, as every thinking man must, that, irrespective of position in life, there are some persons who are born with exceptional brain power, and who prefer intellectual pleasures to any other. These were, in his opinion, the true Brahmans.

There are others, again (and these are of course the majority), who are willing to do

their duty in so far as they see it, but are wholly incapable of abstract thought. Both these classes seemed good in Buddha's eyes, but in a different degree. For the learned minority—the true Brahmans—he instituted an order of mendicants corresponding very closely to the monks of the Romish Church in many particulars. They were to wear a peculiar dress, to live apart from the world, and depend for their sustenance upon charity. They were to procure for themselves the necessities of life, but luxuries were forbidden, and celibacy insisted upon. It must not, however, be supposed from this that Buddha believed in the efficacy either of penance or outward forms; what he wished to do was to bring about the happiness of his followers, and although he regarded this life as but a preparation for a better one, yet he wished his mendicant monks to be happy even here, provided only that their progress was not retarded.

It was, as we have seen, Buddha's belief that all sorrow springs from individual life, which is the author of restless desire, hatred, passion, corruption, disease, and all other ills. Our love of personal life, he said, was the

result of egotism, and this egotism must be destroyed before we can hope to arrive at Nirvāna. In this he agreed with the Hindus generally, but his method of abolishing this sinful lust after life, as it was called, was entirely new. He had himself experienced the fact that penance and mortification do not necessarily produce a calm and holy state of mind, but, on the contrary, it often makes a man crave all the more for the ordinary comforts of life. Therefore the mendicants were taught to satisfy in moderation their requirements, and when they had slept, washed, dressed, and partaken of food, they were thought to be in the most favourable condition for intellectual work. Luxuries were only forbidden to the mendicants because they were supposed to foster a love of individual life, and to attract the mind away from higher things.

Although Buddha made these and other rules, he did not attribute the smallest value upon them as mere outward observances. The shaving of the head, the wearing of the orange robe, abstinence from intoxicating liquors,—these and similar prescribed forms had no virtue to impart to him who observed them, they were simply the means by which it was thought that man could best attain to the crowning triumph of life—the mastery over self, and the annihilation of egotism. I have said that Buddha desired the mendicants to be happy in any way that did not encourage the lust of life. What kind of happiness, then, was open to them? It was intellectual knowledge, love for others, and contemplation.

Cold and unattractive as this may seem to us, to many Buddhists it was as the breath of heaven. We must remember, that in old days life was a perpetual struggle, unrelieved by many of the arts of civilization or seasons of peaceful prosperity. To men of quiet, reflective minds, therefore, there must have been much to sicken them of the turmoil, the ostentation, and the coercive practices of ordinary life. To them it must have seemed a beautiful religion, which enabled a man to live apart from the world and indifferent to its excitements. How pleasant to think that the restless, weary, and disappointed could cast off the trials and anxieties which clogged their progress, and breathe an atmosphere of mental serenity and peace.

Even in the present prosaic age it is generally acknowledged that the highest pleasures are those which "carry one out of oneself," as the expression is, and how much more must men less happily circumstanced than ourselves have prized a form of happiness which no tyrant could wring from them, no adversity deprive them. To those whose lives are busy, and who spend but little time in contemplation, it may seem impossible to derive any pleasure from a philosophy in which the annihilation of self is the main feature. To us the very idea of pleasure implies personal, individual gratification, but the fact is, that even we do forget for the time being the circumstances which surround us, and the individual cares and anxieties which press upon us.

The Buddhists felt this just the same, but in a far greater degree. Owing to their climate and other material circumstances, the Hindus were (and are still) more prone to silent thought and meditation than are the inhabitants of colder countries, and they were therefore well able to grasp the inner meaning of Buddha's teaching.

The life of the Buddhist mendicant,

although simple and monotonous, was not without its periods of activity. He was bound to wash, clean his hut, collect his daily food in his alms-bowl, and to study certain books, besides finding time to meditate. There were five principal subjects for meditation, namely, love, pity, joy, impurity, serenity!

As these five subjects contain the whole essence of Buddha's philosophy, it may be well, perhaps, for us to consider them separately.

## CHAPTER XII.

THE subject for the first meditation was love, a subject which has been talked and written about for so many centuries that it may well seem to us to be one with which we are well acquainted ; but we shall see that love, from the Buddhist's point of view, presents an aspect which is most unfamiliar.

The love of the Buddhist mendicant was not that of the young man for the maiden, nor that of brother for brother, nor yet was it that universal feeling of kindliness towards all men which is supposed to be the prevailing characteristic of the philanthropist. Love was the Buddhist's religion ! In their opinion hatred was painful, whilst intense love was the highest of all joys, and made them worthy of Nirvāna. This exalted passion can only be described as close spiritual sympathy, and a longing for that perfect union with the ideal which could only take place when the individual, as such, existed no more. The Buddhist might love one person more than another, because the ideal is more perceptible in some than in others. Appearances, manners, and habits were regarded as mere outward coverings; but at the same time, by means of these, it was possible to divine whether the immortal spark within was being developed, or whether it was suffered to stagnate beneath a load of vulgar and sordid passions. Therefore the Buddhist could reverence those superior beings who had grown indifferent to earthly considerations; he could keenly sympathize with those on the same level as himself, who were still struggling upward, and he could be not merely tolerant, but full of compassion for those whose spiritual emanations were imprisoned in an earthly character so low as to be lost to recognition. Even the most degraded animals were treated with tenderness, for the sake of what lay enshrouded in the coarse and bestial frame. There was ample material, then, for the meditation of the devotee when he fixed his thoughts upon love. There were times when he had to rid himself of all recollection of his own troubles, and to enter fully into those of others. Times when he must think of the sinful, the ignorant, the unhappy, and learn to find excuse even for those failings which he had himself been able to avoid. There were times when he must look upward to those enlightened ones whom he believed to be treading their last course with earthly feet, and whose angel wings were half unfolded, ready to bear them to another sphere. Lastly, there were times when the Buddhist must think of love as the ideal of all spiritual union and happiness, the crown of his life's desire. I know not how to put into words the full meaning of love in its unindividualized aspect—as a religion. To most of us the idea of love is so personal, that we can scarcely hear or speak the word without mentally photographing, as it were, from memory, the faces and forms of those most dear to us. The well-known countenance, the oft-heard voice, the long-familiar peculiarities become so endeared to us through associations with the person to whom they belong, that it seems impossible to dissociate the idea of love from some kind of physical individuality. We may, however, be aided by the use of an illustration. When a friend is long absent from us, we treasure their picture, and look upon it so often that every line is familiar, and even its setting becomes dear to us. But when that friend returns to us we no longer need his portrait; the image is superfluous beside the reality.

In the same manner love as an idea is related to love personalized. Hence in this world we can only feel love when it has been imaged in some person or thing, but when earthly life has passed away, it is conceivable that we might recognize the "thing in itself," the idea in its pristine splendour. Such must have been the opinion of Buddha, and of the purest of his disciples, because love in the ordinary sense of the word could never have been so highly esteemed by a sect who set so little value upon individual life. The pious Buddhist could not grow more and more indifferent to earth if it contained all that he loved, and from whom death must separate him at least for a time. But if, on the other hand, he believed that dear though some individuals might be, the distinction of "I and thou" was not a bridge, but a barrier between him and them, an obstacle to true union of spirit, he would then long all the more for his emancipation from the body, and await with hope the angel of death, whom he would picture not as a destroyer, but rather as an analyst, to come and separate the immortal from the mortal, the incorruptible from the corrupt, the everlasting truth from the transitory illusion.

The next subject for meditation—pity—is one which requires but little explanation, except to say that in the Buddhist philosophy it was not akin to contempt.

Joy was the third meditation. In it the mendicant was bidden to reflect upon the joys of others, and to rejoice with them, as he had sympathized with the sad. This was Buddha's method of annihilating egotism.

Fourthly, the mendicant was to meditate upon impurity. Under this head all bodily suffering, disease, vice, ignorance, and folly were classed; and by reflecting on these he would perceive how imperfect is life, how transient its pleasures, compared with its pains, and how quickly the purest and most beautiful earthly product must yield itself up to decay and corruption.

Serenity is the last meditation for the

Buddhist, who is then to think of all those things which men prize in this world, such as honour, fame, riches, beauty, and dominion, and strive to regard them with indifference. The Buddhist's treasure was not to be laid up in this world, and he was to care nothing for the mad infatuations of the hour. Thus, above the reach of all tumult, though accessible, through sympathy, to every shade of joy and sorrow, the mendicant was bound to pass through life with quiet dignity, and to be ready, when the time came, to quit it without a shadow either of fear or of regret.

The philosophy of Buddha also adapted itself to those who were not suited either by intellect or disposition to become monks. These were permitted to enter upon almost all those enjoyments of life which are usually considered innocent. They were to be honest, truthful, constant to one wife, kindly in manner and speech, sober, diligent in business, and so forth; but, on the other hand, they were allowed to enjoy domestic life and hospitality, and to make use of the comforts or luxuries which fortune might place within their reach. We must not forget that Buddha believed the true object of life to be happiness, and that although he considered the highest happiness could only be obtained by renunciation of the world, he forced this course upon no one. It was of no use for a man to turn monk except through natural inclination, and the upright householder might still progress along the heavenly way, although afar off. In short, Buddha seems to have regarded the innocent pleasures of life as a parent regards the toys of his children. He knows that the love for these must die out before manhood can be reached, but frivolous though the childish games appear, he does not prohibit them. He is aware that to take away the toys would be to inflict pain without producing the desired development of mind, and so he is content to wait until the time comes when the children will abandon their pastimes of their own accord, because they have grown too old to find pleasure in them.

# CHAPTER XIII.

THIS last chapter has been reserved for the examination of the future states, promised by the three forms of Hinduism which we have been reviewing.

Pantheistic Hinduism, as described in Part I., taught, that man should ultimately be absorbed into Brahma, but as their notions of Brahma were somewhat nebulous and indefinite, their visions of this consummation could not have been very distinct. Inasmuch, however, as they regarded him as a personal deity, they probably supposed that man would become one with him, sharing his rule, and the splendour of his existence.

The Vedantists, on the other hand, denied that Brahma had a personal existence, and therefore their idea of absorption into him must have been something widely different. It was, in fact, an ideal state of consciousness, necessitating total loss of individuality. In this we see how Buddha, though separate from, yet ran parallel with Vedantism, for his Nirvāna and the Vedantist absorption seem to have meant exactly the same thing. Both systems of philosophy appear to have agreed in substance, but differed in the words used. Buddha, using the word soul in the old orthodox sense, denied its existence; whilst Vedantism, probably for form's sake, retained the word, but divested it of the meaning previously assigned to it. In the same way the two systems differed verbally concerning Brahma.

Buddha regarded this name in its orthodox sense (signifying a personal deity), and said that no such person as Brahma existed; whereas the Vedantists believed in Brahma, but stripped him of all personal powers and attributes. The Nirvāna of Buddha, therefore, and the Brahma of the Vedanta meant precisely the same thing. We are told by Professor Max Müller, that "if we look in the Dhamma-pada at every passage where Nirvāna is mentioned, there is not one which would require that its meaning should be annihilation, whilst most, if not all, would become perfectly unintelligible, if we assigned to the word Nirvāna that signification." Many other authorities on Indian religions also hold the same opinion, and therefore, although no absolute proof can be furnished, I think we can have little doubt but that entrance upon Nirvāna was merely a new expression in place of absorption into Brahma; that is to say, both signified the loss of individuality, and the realization of ideal happiness.

Such notions of happiness are so entirely at variance with the views which we of the nineteenth century instinctively hold, that we are apt to think the heaven of the Hindus (whether Vedantist or Buddhist) was very little better than complete annihilation. How, we are inclined to ask, can a man be happy if his individuality is lost? or rather, how can a man, in such a case, be said to exist at all? The question is so difficult, and we can understand so little of the working of the Hindu mind in old days, that I cannot attempt to say for certain what Nirvāna or absorption really meant, or where the attraction in them lay; but I am so sure that these states did not signify annihilation, that in default of more certain information, I give what might very well be a picture of this consummation of happiness for which the pious Hindus were willing to work, to wait, and to die. I believe that if one of these had been questioned, he might have replied somewhat as follows—

"I believe that the mainspring of my life is a divine emanation, a spark from the perfect flame which burns for ever. This emanation, itself containing the elements of pure love, consciousness, and knowledge, became imprisoned in matter, became the life of this earthly body, and I, as an individual, was produced.

"My intellect and personality are temporal, and entirely dependent on the body. By the aid of mutable reason, the immutable cause of life becomes conscious of itself, and thus the man may work out his own redemption from the prison-house of the body. I believe that I shall pass through a series of transmigrations, and that although my character will depend upon circumstances, and vary with each birth, the divine portion of me will enter upon a new life in precisely that state of bondage or emancipation in which it quitted the old one; but wherever or whatever I may be, I must ultimately work my way upwards. At last the time will come when I shall be freed from all egotism, all lust of life, all material desires, and I shall long only to join the ideal from whence I came. When I enter upon Nirvāna I shall lose all consciousness of I and thou, but I shall be profoundly conscious of love, joy, and peace. The divine thread of consciousness which will have run through all past ages, will not desert me when I attain to the light from whence all consciousness has been derived. I shall still feel, although recollection of self will be lost, just as on earth a man may abrogate himself through love. The greatest happiness I have ever known in the world has been at times when I have been so filled with love and adoration that for a time I have become oblivious of myself and my environment. Such intensity of feeling shall be mine, only deeper and more precious than I can ever dream, when I lose myself in light. Then shall I have cognizance of the *realities* in their pristine splendour, of which the beauties of earth are but finite and broken reflections ; there shall I meet all the spirits I have ever known and loved, and I shall rush to meet them as the rivers rush toward the sea. I shall not perceive them as with mortal eyes, nor hear their voices as with mortal ears, but I shall feel their presence as my own. Our communion will not be one of sympathy, which is only kinship, but one of absolute unity, as the colours live and mingle in one dazzling gem! So shall we be throughout the ages—motionless, desireless, changeless, and serene; for though time be a portion of eternity, eternity does not consist of portions of time. The intense joy of the present, therefore, shall exist for everlasting ages, and the long, long vista of for ever shall flash like a lightning gleam!"

THE END.